I'm not crazy, I'm just weird

Margaret Sheekey

Presentation by *BookLeaf Publishing*

Web: www.bookleafpub.com

E-mail: info@bookleafpub.com

ISBN: 9789358313512

First edition 2023

To my family and my friends

Thank you for letting me be myself

PREFACE

For all the weirdos.

Phoenix

From the ashes I
Stretch, and start unveiling my
Flaming, golden wings.

Rhyming Spiral

Today I felt like rhyming,
To help me fix my timing.
Because when I come to work too early,
My thoughts can go all twirly
And
Spiral
Spiral
Spiral
Down into a ball of anxiety,
About my notoriety
Do I come across as too tough?
Am I even good enough?
Perhaps it's best if I disappeared.
Am I crazy? Or just weird?
But
No
No
No
You're better than you think you are!
You are your own shining star!

The Little Dragon

There once was
a little dragon
who had to wear a helmet when flying.

She was a
quite clumsy dragon
and wore it to feel safer.

One day she fell
and hit her head.
This left a scar under her chin.

She got scared when
the other dragons
flew past her too fast.

She got scared when
the other dragons
blocked her path.

But sometimes,
a kind dragon would
let her through and give her space.
And she felt more confident.
And she kept on flying.

Ghosts have feelings too

You don't see us,
You just read our words,
But ghosts have feelings too.

You just hear our voices,
You don't see our faces,
But ghosts have feelings too.

Sometimes you ask us how we are,
But you don't really care.
You just want something from us.
But ghosts have feelings too.

We know that you are struggling,
That you are busy, you are tired, you are
stressed.
We know you don't want to let anyone down,
Your bosses, your colleagues, your patients.
We understand.
Because ghosts have feelings too.

Tiger

Tiger, Tiger, burning bright,
Make me strong so I can fight.
Teach me how to camouflage
And how to not self-sabotage.
Tiger, Tiger, burning bright,
Keep me safe with all your might.

Supermarket Thoughts

Sometimes I like to think,
That there's a small man in the till,
Making the beeping noise.

A remarkable bright creature

I wish I was an octopus,
Floating in the sea,
Drifting along the sea bed,
With no responsibilities.

I'd make a little garden,
And hide in tiny spaces.
I'd float my eight legs all around,
And give the best embraces.

But if I was on the land,
And still in octopus form,
I could carry all the shopping in at once,
Do the hoovering at the same time as the
dusting,
Do some typing, whilst I'm writing,
And unblock toilets with my flexible suckered
arm.

So if I was an octopus,
I'd stay within the sea,
Wafting in the currents,
And I can just be me.

Atticus

I think that Atticus Finch
Is an example of
A perfect Libra.

He is tactful,
And diplomatic,
And can fit in with any crowd.

He strives for fairness,
And lives for justice.
A personification of Themis.

He does overthink.
But knows exactly the right thing to say,
At the right time.

A true Libra.

La Luna

When I'm driving,
Or walking on my own at night,
I like to look up and see the moon.
She makes me feel protected,
Always watching,
Reflecting light.
A maternal figure,
Making me feel safe,
And not so alone.

Mornings by the Sea

I like early mornings.
Seeing the many colours of the morning,
The yellows, oranges and pinks,
Before the sun rises.
When the sea is still, cold and refreshing.
All is calm and all is peaceful.
The fish are jumping,
The mermaids are singing,
And sometimes the moon is still there to say
goodbye.

I also like it when the wind is here,
And the sea is choppy.
The sirens are calling,
The seagulls are screeching.
I'm jumping through the waves.
It's invigorating,
And I feel alive.

Definition

When I turned thirty,
I realised that I had spent my entire twenties
Studying and working in medicine.

Whilst I am proud of my achievements,
I didn't want "being a doctor" to define me.
I wanted more for me
And for my life.

So I decided to be more creative,
Try some poetry, be a poet.

I decided to travel more,
See the world, be an explorer.

I decided to try new things,
Say yes, be a go-getter.

Now there are more ways to define me,
Not just the prefix before my name.

Marty

My best friend's name is Marty,
He's a very special dog.
He gives me love and kindness
And clears up my brain fog.

He thinks he's very clever,
When he steals and hides my shoes.
He does it so I can never leave,
And leave him feeling blue.

We enjoy each other's company,
We can be still together for hours.
We have our own special games,
There'll never be a friendship like ours.

Running in the rain by the sea

I like to run.
It helps me clear my head when I feel frustrated,
When I feel stressed,
When I feel foggy.

I like to run in the rain.
I like that feeling of clarity combined with the
cleansing power of the rain.
It soothes me,
It clears my mind,
An extra challenge to overcome.

I like to run in the rain by the sea.
To hear the crashing waves and feel the sea
breeze,
I find it invigorating,
I find it freeing,
A powerful view to spur me on
And continue my journey.

Mutual Connections on a Train Journey

I saw a tall horse,
Calmly grazing in a field,
As the train went past.

The tall horse saw me,
Looking through the train window,
Calmly sitting down.

I saw another horse,
Playing with a tricycle,
In a different field.

The other horse saw me,
Studied my face carefully,
As I looked perplexed.

On the platform I
Saw a man's trousers falling,
Stopping at his knees.

This man ignored me.
I think he was embarrassed,
That we saw his pants.

Ode to Iris

Rosy cheeks on a frostbitten morning.
Autumn leaves on the trees, adorning.
Irises margining Europe's waterways.
Neon lights saying "go", on our highways.
Bodies of water, crashing under the sun.
Oh, but an aubergine, isn't quite one.
Wisteria, another flower, now we are done.

The Cave

I went into the cave to discover transmutation.
As I stepped into the dark, I barely noticed the
dripping.
The many droplets of water, falling from the
stalactites,
Fell onto me,
But I didn't notice.
I was numb.
I couldn't see anything around me.
I couldn't make out any shapes.
My brain couldn't take it.

So I stopped.
I gave myself a break.
I let my eyes adjust.
I gave myself time for me.

Slowly I began to see,
My mind becoming clearer.
The iridescent walls of the cave,
I could finally appreciate.

I continued my journey,
Out through the end of the cave.
Physically I looked similar,

Perhaps a little slimmer, the shadows had grown
under my eyes.

But internally,
I knew I had changed.
I was stronger,
And I was free.

Peacock

The peacock fans his
Feathers out behind his back,
Looking very sharp.

Emeralds and blues.
Multiple eyes at the ends.
Jewel tones work for him.

The Journey

The Fool went on his journey,
And met the great Magician.
He gave the Fool blind courage,
To help him on his mission.

The High Priestess stopped him,
To give him further wisdom.
He later saw the Empress,
And discovered his reproductive system.

The Emperor was not impressed,
When he met this clumsy Fool,
But the Hierophant inspired him,
And he spent some time at his school.

He suddenly fell in Love,
But was not pleased with his choice,
So he jumped upon the Chariot,
In order to find his voice.

He found his inner Strength,
When he calmed the lion without a groan,
And carried on as the Hermit.
On this next path, he was alone.

The Wheel of Fortune keeps spinning,
His destiny is within the air.
Justice deals with a sharp sword,
And ensures that our Fool stays fair.

The Hanged Man made the Fool stop
And see things in a different way.
Death transformed the Fool,
And threw him back into the fray.

By the river he found Temperance,
And continued in moderation,
But the Devil then found him,
And let him too temptation.

The lightning crumbled the Tower,
And left the Fool askew.
The Star then gifted hope and faith,
To help the Fool renew.

The Fool then looked towards the Moon,
And started to feel fear.
The Sun then came to warm him up,
To spread happiness, fun and cheer.

Judgement finally reached the Fool,
As he was ready for rebirth.
The Fool had seen the whole World,
He had completed his journey around the Earth.

Dusk

As the sun starts to set,
I enjoy the deeper reds, oranges and purples,
That colour the sky.

As the sun settles lower,
They mix into a deeper purple, navy and black,
And the stars come out.

The stars' light is old.
I don't know if they are still with us,
Their light left many light-years ago.

But I know tomorrow,
The sun will rise again.
The journey continues.

The Swan

This swan decided to follow me.
I don't know why.
I think he just admired who I am as a person.

I was only going for a walk.
"Perhaps he wants to join me" I thought,
"And learn more about humans".
Such a curious swan.

A walking swan is not that graceful,
Compared to when you see them gliding on the water.
They look serene, composed, pure perfection,
Barely breaking the water's surface.

I, however, looked a mess.
Muddy trainers and unkempt hair.

So we walked together,
To learn more about one another,
And learn new customs.

Fin.

There's no such thing as an ending,
Time just keeps extending.

There is no final word,
As we continue undeterred.

It doesn't end when the fat lady sings,
Because the heart keeps beating, and so do other things.

Though if we ask "are there any questions?"
At the end of a presentation,
We are often met with silence,
A solid confirmation that it's over.

www.ingramcontent.com/pod-product-compliance
Lightning Source LLC
LaVergne TN
LVHW010854200726
843508LV00012B/2900